HAL•LEONARD®
KEYBOARD PLAY-ALONG™

1960s ROCK

CONTENTS

T0080088

ISBN 978-1-4234-6185-2

Visit Hal Leonard Online at **www.halleonard.com**

HAL•LEONARD®
CORPORATION
7777 W. BLUEMOUND RD. P.O. BOX 13819
MILWAUKEE, WISCONSIN 53213

Gimme Some Lovin'

Words and Music by Steve Winwood, Muff Winwood and Spencer Davis

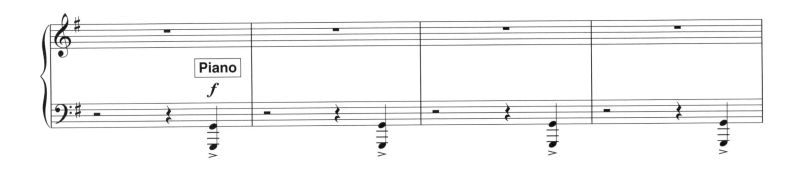

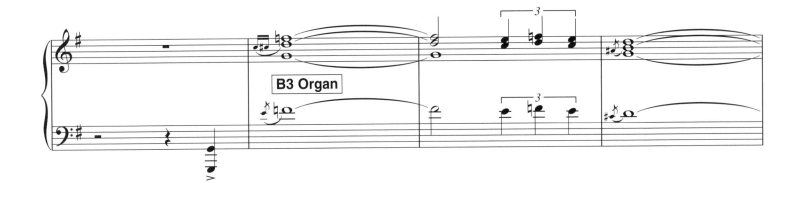

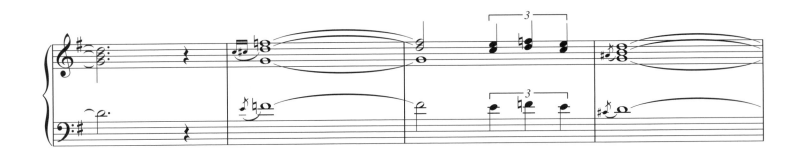

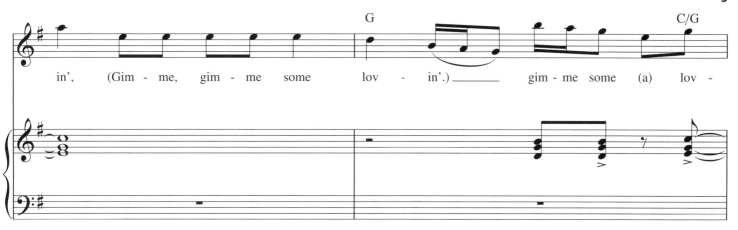

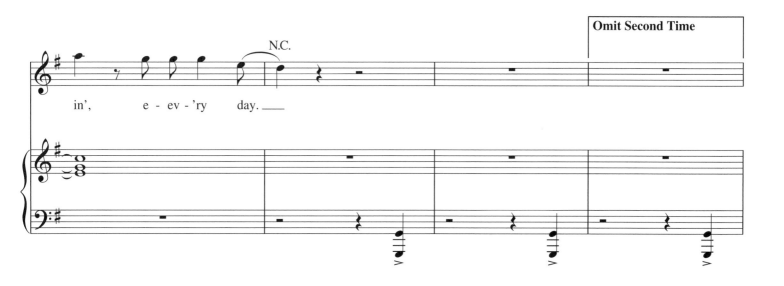

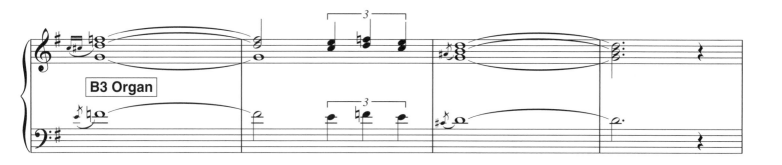

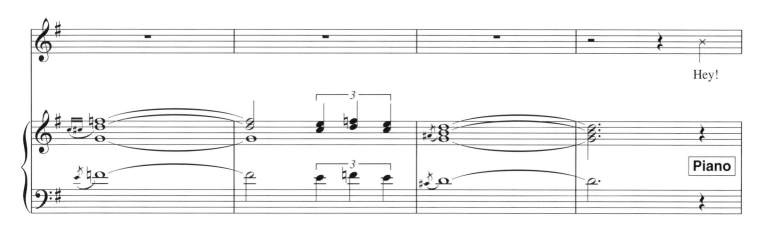

Green Onions

Written by Al Jackson, Jr., Lewis Steinberg,
Booker T. Jones and Steve Cropper

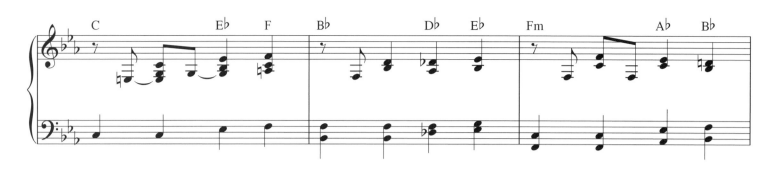

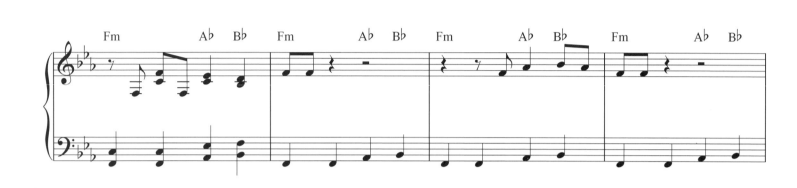

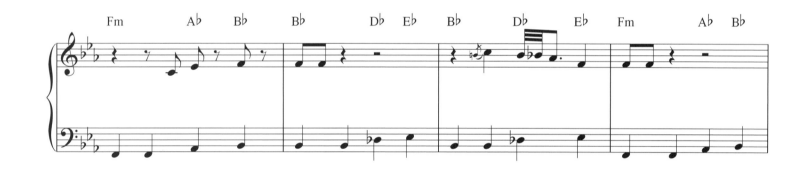

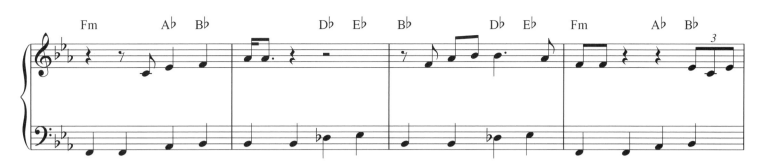

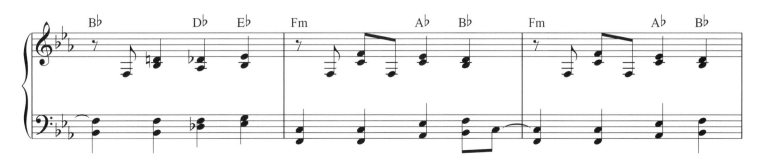

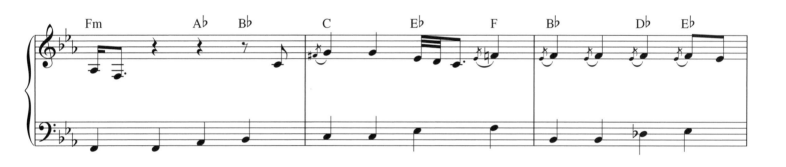

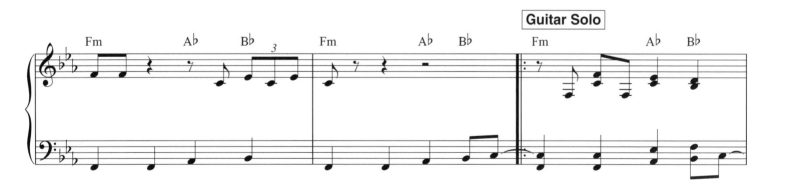

I'm A Believer

Words and Music by
Neil Diamond

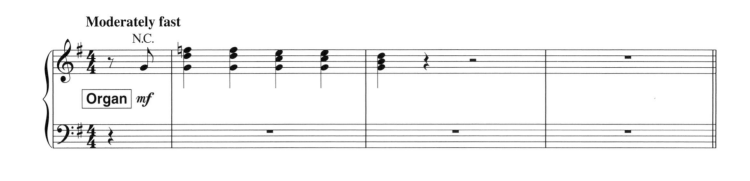

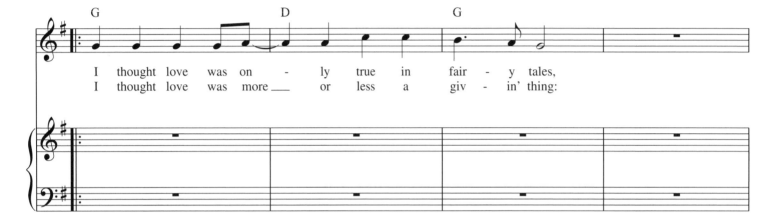

I thought love was on - ly true in fair - y tales,
I thought love was more ___ or less a giv - in' thing:

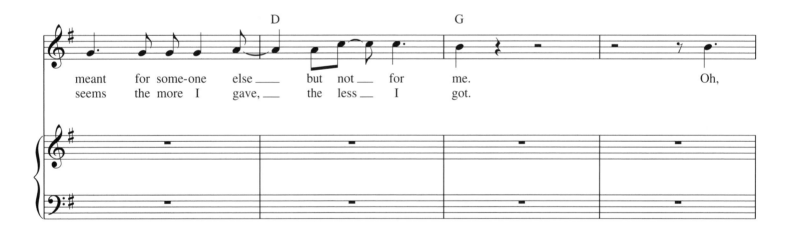

meant for some-one else ___ but not ___ for me.
seems the more I gave, ___ the less ___ I got.

Oh,

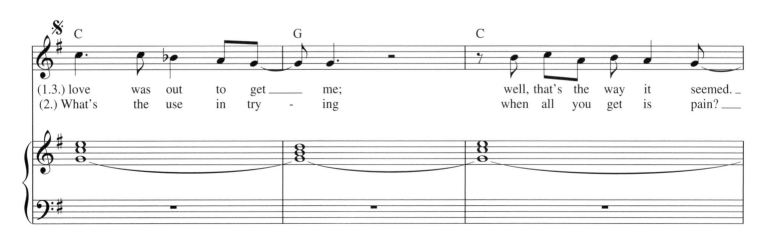

(1.3.) love was out to get ___ me; well, that's the way it seemed. ___
(2.) What's the use in try - ing when all you get is pain? ___

Oh!) I'm a be - liev - er, I could-n't leave ___ her if I tried. ___

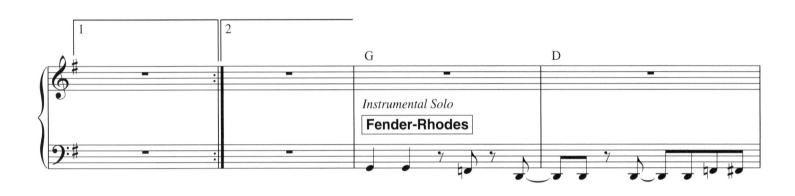

Instrumental Solo
Fender-Rhodes

Oh,
Solo ends

D.S. al Coda

to Organ...

CODA

Yes, I saw her face; ___

Louie, Louie

Words and Music by Richard Berry

Lyrics omitted at the request of the publisher.

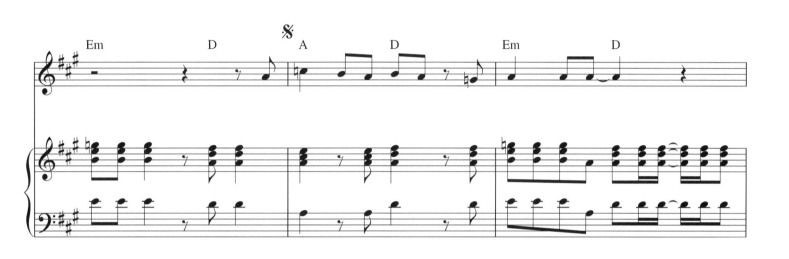

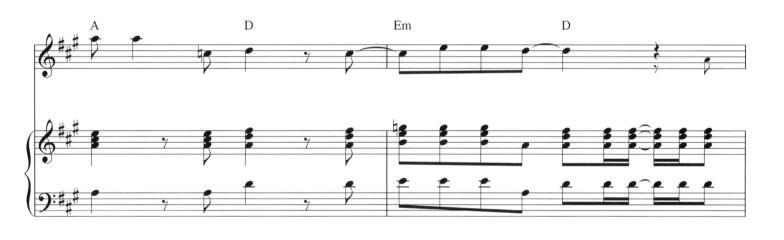

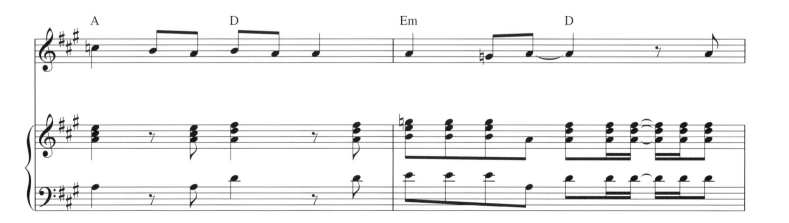

18

Magic Carpet Ride

Words and Music by John Kay and Rushton Moreve

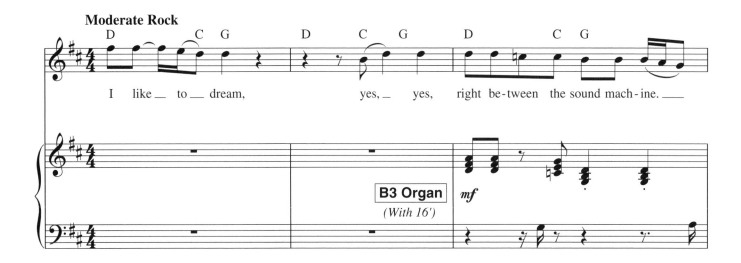

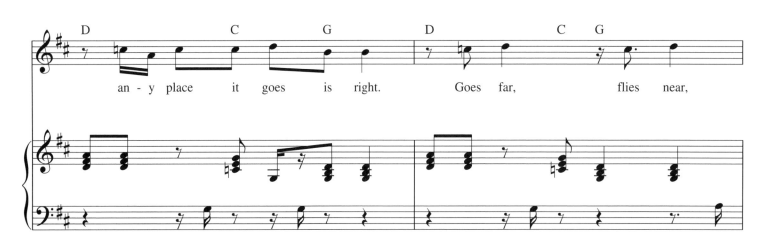

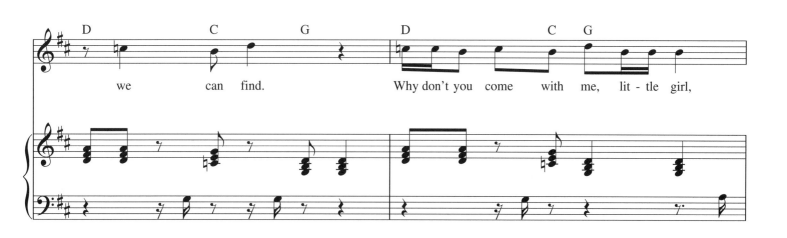

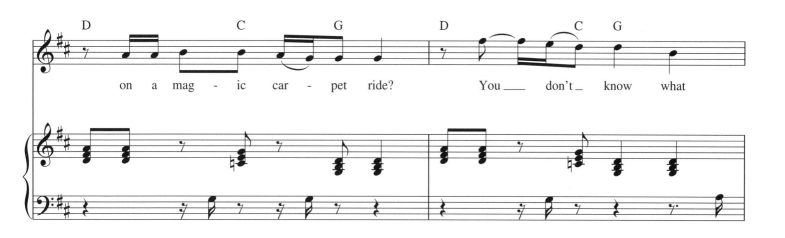

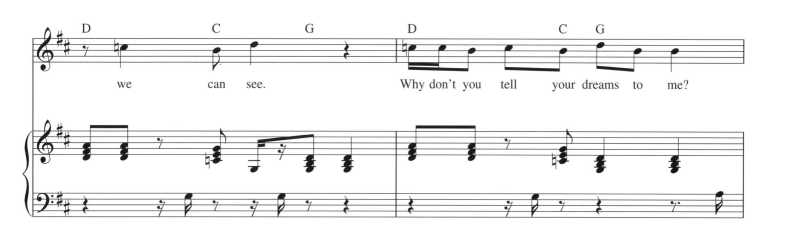

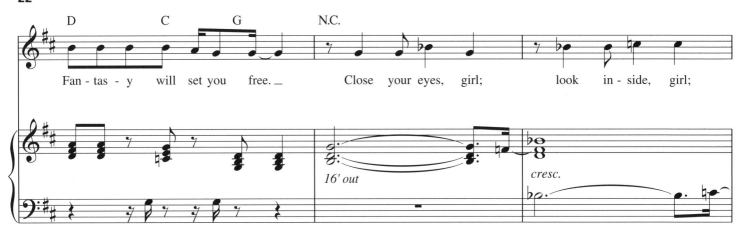

Fan - tas - y will set you free. ___ Close your eyes, girl; look in - side, girl;

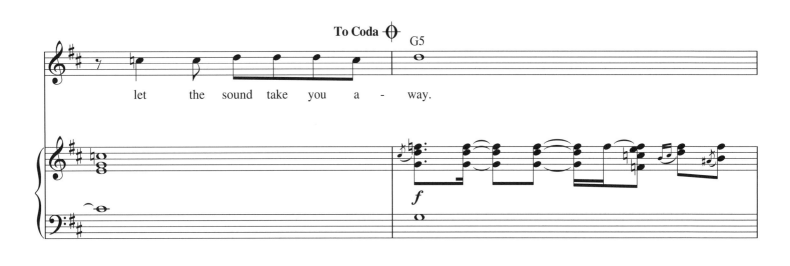

let the sound take you a - way.

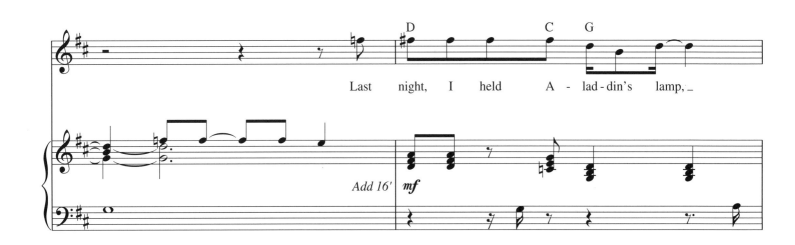

Last night, I held A - lad - din's lamp, ___

and so I wished that I could stay. Be-fore the thing could an-swer me, well,

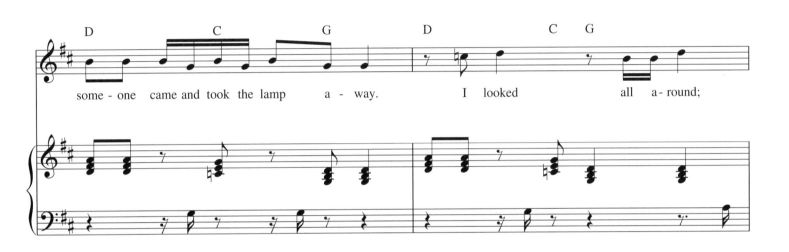

some - one came and took the lamp a - way. I looked all a - round;

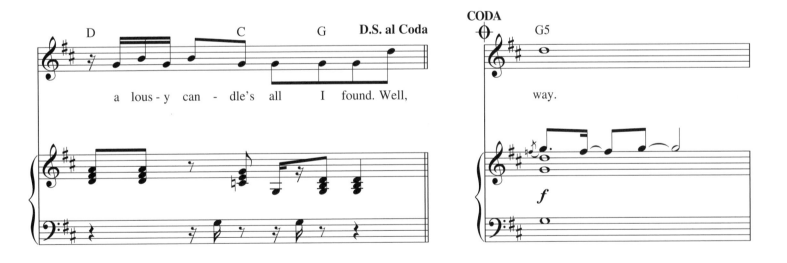

D.S. al Coda

CODA

a lous - y can - dle's all I found. Well, way.

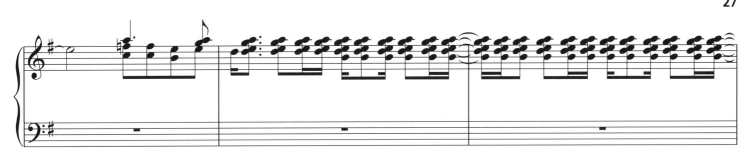

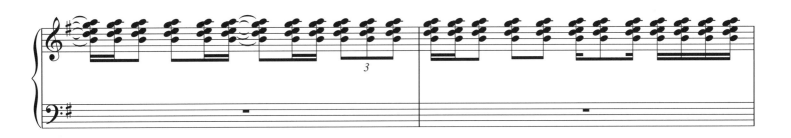

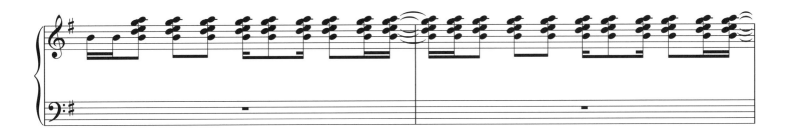

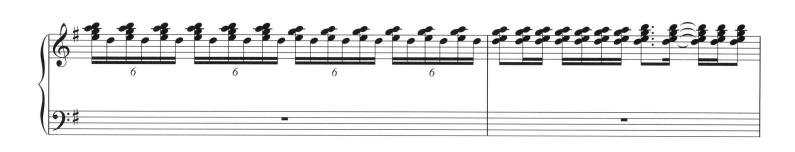

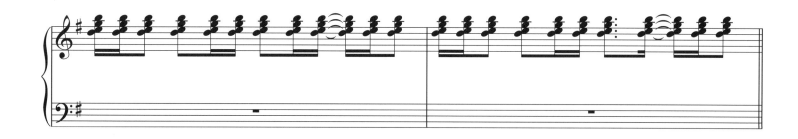

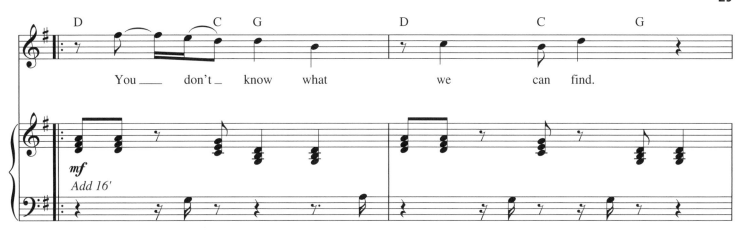

You ___ don't ___ know what we can find.

Why don't you come with me, lit - tle girl, on a mag - ic car - pet ride? Well,

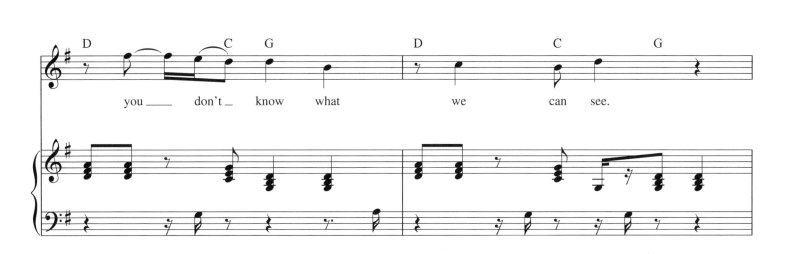

you ___ don't ___ know what we can see.

Repeat and Fade

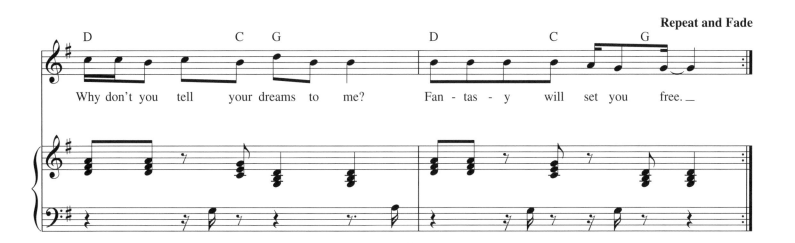

Why don't you tell your dreams to me? Fan - tas - y will set you free. ___

Oh, Pretty Woman

Words and Music by Roy Orbison and Bill Dees

hey.　　　　　　　O - kay;

if that's the way it must be, ___ o - kay. _____

I guess I'll go on home; __ it's late. ___ There'll be to -

mor - row night... But wait, what do I see?

Runaway

Words and Music by Del Shannon and Max Crook

Synth was apparently transposed up a half-step, allowing the glisses to be played on the white keys.

The Twist

Words and Music by Hank Ballard

Take me by ___ my lit - tle hand, ___
We're gon - na twist a, twist a, twist - in'
She real - ly knows ___ how to rock; ___

and go ___ like this.
till we tear the house down.
she knows how to twist.

Ee ___ ah, ___
Come ___ on ___ and
Come ___ on, ___ and

twist; babe, ___ ba - by, twist.
twist; yeah, ___ ba - by, twist.
twist; yeah, ___ ba - by, twist.

Ooh, _

_____ yeah, _____ just ___ like

D.S. al Coda

Yeah, _____   *Solo ends*   you should   see _____

CODA

twist.   Yeah. _

That's ___ al - right. ___

Yeah, _____   twist _

E   B

___ so nice. ___   Twist. _____

A   N.C.   E   N.C.